Angela Gray's
Cookery School

Autumn Recipes

Photographs Huw Jones

Autumn Recipes
Angela Gray's Cookery School
Published in Great Britain in 2018 by
Graffeg Limited

Written by Angela Gray copyright © 2018.
Food photography by Huw Jones
copyright © 2018.
Food styling by Angela Gray.
Designed and produced by Graffeg Limited
copyright © 2018.

Graffeg Limited, 24 Stradey Park Business
Centre, Mwrwg Road, Llangennech,
Llanelli, Carmarthenshire SA14 8YP Wales
UK Tel 01554 824000 www.graffeg.com

ISBN 9781912050437

1 2 3 4 5 6 7 8 9

Photo credits

Pages 6–127, cover and end papers
© Huw Jones

Pages 132, 150–156 © A L S Photography
www.alsphotography.co.uk

Angela Gray's

Cookery School

Autumn Recipes

Photographs Huw Jones

GRAFFEG

Contents

Starters

Mains

Desserts

Preserves

Introduction

Welcome to my autumn kitchen, where an abundance
of seasonal ingredients has inspired the recipes in this
book. From magical fat pumpkins, earthy roots and
irony greens to the wild flavours of game, fungi, fruits
and nuts, the list goes on!

Traditionally this would have been
a particularly busy time of the year
for both professional and home
cooks, as there would be much to do
in both the garden and the kitchen.
As the end of the sultry summer
turned into the golden hues of
autumn, a bumper harvest of home-
grown vegetables and fruits would
need attention. Various preserving
methods would be employed to
extend the variety of foods available
throughout the leaner growing
months ahead.

I am happy to say that this was
very much the tradition in our
house too. In the early years when I

was growing up, half of our garden
was dedicated to flowers and the
other half to vegetables and soft
fruits. Later, when we moved to a
farm, one of the first priorities as a
family was to establish a vegetable
garden. A section of a small field had
been marked out behind our house
ready for sowing. I remember my
stepfather organising us to follow
him with a bag of seed potatoes,
urging us to drop them into the
trench he was forming ahead of us
with a rotary hoe.

A couple of years later, we had a
beautiful fruitful garden yielding
healthy crops that needed to be

preserved. This was the way I came to understand what each season would bring to the table. My education extended into the kitchen, where my mum would make pickles, chutneys, jams and jellies. The presence of wild game and fish were also commonplace in our kitchen courtesy of my stepfather's passion for outdoor pursuits.

We also went foraging as a family and sometimes with friends, spending endless hours picking blackberries, damsons, sloes, rosehips, cobnuts and mushrooms. A particular outing I recall was when we stopped abruptly on the way back from an outing to Porthcawl; a field had been spotted, dotted with what looked like large cotton wool balls. They turned out to be field mushrooms the size of saucers! We picked a good few and had them for supper on toast, simply fried in butter.

I have paid homage to those beautiful fungi in this book and have included a grown-up version of mushrooms on toast. Fungi are fascinating, beautiful and a little mysterious. You can encounter so many on autumnal woodland walks, poking out from under damp fallen leaves or fused to the bark of ancient trees. However, you must know what and what not to pick!

I have used a few varieties in some of my recipes, including porcine, portobello and truffle in the Agnolotti – lovely filled pasta pouches and little tight chestnut mushrooms in the Welsh beef in ale with Yorkshire puddings.

There is much to look forward to, including adaptations of recipes from my travels around the world, such as a delicious Lebanese vegetable kibbeh. From Italy, a beautiful, full-flavoured Roman-style chicken with saffron, honey, figs and grapes.

There are also my essential weekend snacks like shakshuka, a spicy one-pot egg dish from the Middle East, and lahmacun, a Turkish flat bread topped with meat and aromatic spices. Both are perfect for setting you up for the day and taking care of that much-needed spice fix.

I also must mention an old favourite, the good old-fashioned jacket spud, but with a difference in my Greedy Baked Potatoes, overfilled and oozing with seasonal flavour. Other revisited dishes include salt duck, bourride, and steamed lemon puddings, which reflect the style of cuisine I served in my restaurant days. Very eclectic!

I always feel a different energy at this time of year, a natural determination to be busy, probably stemming from a discipline to make the most of everything in the moment, instilled in me all those years ago. That fruitful garden, the bumper harvests all picked and ready to preserve, or to be made into recipes and frozen. Writing this book has helped me realise that.

When I was testing some of the recipes at home, I sensed a particular atmosphere; the evenings were drawing in and that first real chill in the air had arrived. I felt a cosy, warm and nurturing feeling, and a need to feed people! There was so much food!

Well, my table is set and the candles are lit as twilight falls. The aroma of sweet spices permeates the air as I gently heat my Malabar chicken curry and vada (little split pea cakes). Dessert, the baked apples with caramel sauce, are done and just need to be popped in the oven. All I need to do is greet my friends with a little theatre. I will cook poori breads and watch their faces as they balloon in front of their eyes! As supper is served I know this will be the first of many to come throughout the generous months of autumn.

Angela Gray

Spiced Butternut Velouté with Crab Salad

Ingredients

25g butter

1 dessertspoon light olive oil

450g squash, peeled and cubed

200g potatoes, peeled and cubed

1 medium onion, peeled and sliced

1 small leek, trimmed and chopped

1 bay leaf

1 rounded teaspoon sea salt

½ teaspoon black pepper

1 walnut-size piece ginger, peeled and finely chopped

2 fat garlic cloves, grated to a paste

½ teaspoon ground cinnamon

1 teaspoon fennel seeds

¼ teaspoon ground cumin

½ teaspoon ground coriander

1 small chilli, finely chopped – seeds removed for a milder finish

1L vegetable or chicken stock

150g crème fraîche

A squeeze or two of lemon juice to finish

Serves 6

What you do

1 Melt the butter in a saucepan, add the oil, then the squash, potato and onion and stir through.

2 Add about 100ml of water and put a lid on the pan. Cook for about 7–10 minutes until the onion is soft.

3 Remove the lid, add the leek, bay leaf, seasoning, ginger, garlic, spices and chilli and cook for about 2 minutes, adding a little water to keep the spices in a paste-like consistency.

4 Pour in the stock, bring to the boil and then reduce to a simmer. Cook until the vegetables are soft.

5 Blitz in a food processor until smooth, stir in the crème fraîche, taste and adjust the seasoning to your liking, adding a little lemon juice to balance the sweetness of the squash and onion.

Crab Salad

Ingredients

2 garlic cloves, peeled, finely chopped and then pasted using $\frac{1}{2}$ teaspoon sea salt and your kitchen knife

1 small bunch of coriander, roots and stems only, washed and finely chopped

1 green bird's eye chilli, finely chopped (or more to taste if you like it hot)

2 tablespoons palm sugar

2 tablespoons fish sauce

3 tablespoons lime juice, more if you like it citrusy

2 shallots, peeled and finely chopped

300g fresh white crab meat – 25% brown meat mixed in is delicious

Coriander leaves and a few drops of chilli oil

What you do

1 To make the crab salad, simply mix everything except the crab together in a bowl, cover and chill.

2 When ready to serve, mix in the 300g of fresh crab and leave to infuse for 10 minutes. Spoon the crab into the centre of 6 warmed soup bowls and pour the butternut velouté around.

3 Finish with a little chopped coriander leaf and a few spots of chilli oil.

Potted Rabbit with Pancetta

This is such a lovely, deliciously rich and flavourful dish. You can use other pieces of game meat such as pheasant and duck legs. The pork will keep everything moist and palatable.

Ingredients

450g fatty pork belly

1 rabbit, jointed, about 900g

75g pancetta, cut into lardoons/strips

2 bay leaves

4 sprigs thyme

1 stick celery, cut into 4

1 medium head of garlic, cut in half

2 shallots, skins removed and halved

12 juniper berries, bashed

¼ teaspoon ground mace

1 teaspoon sea salt

½ teaspoon black pepper

300ml dry cider

Water

2 teaspoons Dijon mustard

250g unsalted butter

Serves 4–8

What you do

1 Heat the oven to 220°C/Fan 200°C/Gas 7.

2 Make a bed of pork belly in a large casserole dish, place the joints of rabbit and the pancetta on top and cover with the remaining pork belly.

3 Tuck in the bay, thyme, celery, garlic, shallots and juniper around the meats. Pour in the cider and enough water to cover the meat. Cover with a lid or foil and roast for 30 minutes, then turn down the heat to 140°C/Fan 120°C/Gas 1 and cook for 2 ½ hours, until the rabbit is tender and can be shredded with a fork.

4 Remove from the oven and leave until cool enough to handle. Pull all the rabbit meat off the bones onto a board or a plate and shred with a pair of forks or your hands.

⑤ Transfer the meat to a large bowl. Shred the pork in the same way and add to the rabbit. Work the two meats together, crushing the pork fat thoroughly into the mix so it is evenly spread. Add the salt, pepper, mace and Dijon mustard. Mix well and moisten with a ladle of the cooking liquor.

⑥ To seal the meat, melt the butter over a low heat then pack the meat into sterilised jars, pressing down with the back of a spoon to push out any air pockets. Leave 1cm of space at the top of the jars. Line a sieve with a piece of muslin or a J-cloth, boil the kettle and pour the water through. Next, pour the liquefied butter through into a small bowl; this will clarify it, removing any milk solids. Spoon the clarified butter on top of the meat in each jar.

⑦ Place the lids on and store your potted meats in the fridge. Leave for at least a week before eating. They will keep for a couple of months, but once the seal has been broken you should use within a couple of days.

Note – Always bring the potted meat to room temperature before serving. That way it will be a good consistency for spreading thickly onto hot toast and the flavours will be full.

I serve this in ramekins lined with cling film so they are easy to pop out when ready to serve, or, for a nice touch, look out for some small individual clip jars – 125ml sizes are perfect and will make 8 for a supper party. Alternatively, make 4 x 250ml jars, or 2 x 500ml jars.

Autumn
Nut Pesto

19

Ingredients

400ml olive oil

100g hazelnuts

100g walnuts

100g almonds

4 garlic cloves, sliced

1 small bunch sage, about 24 leaves

5 sprigs rosemary, fonds

6 wide strips lemon zest, removed with a peeler

2 wide strips orange zest, removed with a peeler

1 teaspoon sea salt

½ teaspoon black pepper

100g chestnuts

1 small bunch parsley, chopped

200g Parmesan cheese

4 tablespoons lemon juice – depending on your taste

Makes 500ml

What you do

1 Warm the olive oil in a large pan, add the nuts, garlic, sage leaves, rosemary fonds, lemon and orange zest. Poach for 10 minutes then add the salt, pepper, chestnuts and chopped parsley. Leave to cool.

2 Place in a processor, add the cheese and blitz to form a loose pesto. Taste and adjust the seasoning, sharpening with a little lemon juice.

3 Store in airtight jars, add a thin layer of olive oil and chill.

This is delicious served with pasta, game, or as a stuffing for various meats. Just add some breadcrumbs to bind it into a firmer mixture and stuff it under chicken breast skin, inside a pork tenderloin or into field mushrooms and roast.

Ribollita

This is a regular lunch dish at our autumn Italian Kitchen course. People are always surprised at how delicious and filling it is! The secret to achieving great results is to take your time throughout the cooking process to concentrate the flavours. Seasoning is also important, so taste as you go along to ensure a rich, balanced finish.

Ingredients

4 tablespoons olive oil

2 medium onions, peeled and diced

2 large carrots, peeled and diced

3 sticks celery, ribs peeled with a vegetable peeler, cut into sticks, then diced

3 large garlic cloves, peeled and finely chopped or grated

1 bay leaf

1 level teaspoon fennel seeds

½ teaspoon chilli flakes

400g can chopped tomatoes

250g dried cannellini beans

300g cavolo nero/black kale, ribs removed and coarsely shredded

1 teaspoon sea salt

¼ teaspoon black pepper

4 thick slices of bread, sourdough brings added flavour

Topping

100g fried chopped pancetta

Mixed with:

6 tablespoons olive oil

3 tablespoons lemon juice

1 teaspoon fennel seeds

1 teaspoon chilli flakes

1 teaspoon thyme leaves, chopped

Chopped parsley to finish

Serves 4-6

What you do

1 To cook the beans, soak them in plenty of water overnight. Drain, rinse and tip into a saucepan, cover with water and add a couple of slices of onion, a cracked garlic clove and some celery leaves if you have them. Boil, then simmer until soft through. Leave to cool in the liquid.

2 To make the ribollita, heat the olive oil, add the onion, carrot and celery, stir through and sauté gently. Pop a piece of baking parchment directly on top and then a lid. Cook, stirring occasionally until soft and coloured and a little bit sticky – about 20 minutes. Stir in the garlic, bay, fennel and chilli and cook for 1 minute.

3 Stir in the tomatoes and cook until reduced slightly – the mixture should be quite thick – about 10 minutes. Add the cannellini beans with 250ml of their cooking liquid and simmer for 30 minutes.

4 Tear up the slices of bread and add to the pan. Add the cavolo nero or kale and stir in. Simmer for 15–20 minutes, adding a little more bean liquid or stock if needed. Season to your liking.

5 To serve, prepare the topping, ladle the ribollita into warmed bowls, spoon the topping over and sprinkle with chopped parsley.

Tip – A night in the fridge will encourage the flavours to mingle. Keep the vegetable pieces quite small – the soup should be thick, but not a chunky stew. Use a firm white loaf such as a sourdough, torn into rough chunks.

Mushrooms
on Toast

Mushroom foraging is
something I love to do
on a sunny autumn day.
I only pick what I know,
generally field mushrooms,
chanterelle, cepe (porcini)
and boletus.

Ingredients

50g butter

1 teaspoon thyme leaves or sage, finely chopped

1 fat garlic clove, peeled and grated

1 tablespoon brandy (optional)

400g portobello mushrooms, wiped with kitchen paper and thickly sliced

200g shitake mushrooms, wiped and thickly sliced

100g oyster mushrooms, wiped and thickly sliced

1 dessertspoon dried porcini, soaked in a little hot water and then chopped – keep the juice

1 flat teaspoon sea salt

$\frac{1}{4}$ teaspoon black pepper

1–2 teaspoons lemon juice

2 heaped tablespoons crème fraîche

4 large, thick slices of sourdough and butter

Some chopped parsley to serve

Serves 4

What you do

1 Cut the butter into pieces and slowly melt in a large frying pan. Stir in the garlic, turn up the heat and cook for 30 seconds. Add the brandy and flame.

2 Add the mushrooms and stir-fry in the butter. The mushrooms need to remain firm, but a little toasty on the outside.

3 Season with salt and pepper and add 1 teaspoon of lemon juice (taste at the end to see if you need more).

4 Stir in the porcini, the porcini juice and crème fraîche and let the sauce bubble briefly.

5 Remove from the heat, taste and adjust the seasoning.

6 Toast the sourdough and butter liberally. Plate and top with the mushrooms and chopped parsley and serve.

Note – I serve this in many ways; sometimes I add some crumbled chestnuts and slices of apple in with the mushrooms, or a drizzle of truffle oil, a teaspoon of chopped porcini, or a sprinkle of Parmesan.

This recipe is a simple one and remains one of my favourites, inspired by a dish of creamed mushrooms on toast I had in Luxembourg years ago. I never got over it, so created this to take me back.

Salt Duck

I have been making
this recipe for some
years and people
love the flavour and
tenderness of the
duck.

Ingredients

2 Aylesbury-type duck breasts weighing about 350g each

30g coarse sea salt for each breast

1 sprig thyme leaves

1 teaspoon sugar

6 black peppercorns, crushed

Serves 4–6

What you do

1 Mix together the sea salt, thyme leaves, sugar and black peppercorns and rub the meat all over with the mixture.

2 Place the duck breasts skin-side down in a stainless steel, plastic or glass container, cover and keep in the fridge.

3 After 36 hours, turn the breasts over, skin-side up, cover and place in the fridge.

4 After another 36 hours, remove the duck from the fridge and rinse off the salt.

5 Place the duck in a container and cover with cold water.

6 Set your oven at 160°C/ Fan 140°C/Gas 2. Cook the duck uncovered for 40 minutes.

7 Remove the duck breasts from the liquid and leave to cool.

To serve – Thinly slice the duck breasts with or without the fat. Plate a few slices per person with a simple salad of shredded cabbage, sliced eating apple, roasted nuts and a vinaigrette, plus a fruit pickle – the pickled damsons (page 138) or the slow-cooked onions (page 134) are both perfect!

This recipe is adapted from the old traditional Welsh method of curing and was first written in recipe format in Lady Llanover's book *The First Principles of Good Cookery*, published in 1867. It makes a delicious starter served with seasonal leaves and a fruit chutney or pickled fruit.

Sweet Potato Kibbeh

This is the perfect starter to share with friends and family. The irresistible flavours of cheese, tomato and herbs really set the scene for the delicious food to follow.

Ingredients

1kg sweet potatoes

1 medium onion, grated

1 large garlic clove, peeled and grated

1 teaspoon sweet paprika

1 teaspoon cumin seeds

1 teaspoon fennel seeds

1 teaspoon black pepper

2 teaspoons sea salt

4 tablespoons plain flour

350g bulgar wheat – soaked in water for 10 minutes and squeezed out in a cloth

300g mozzarella cheese, shredded

250g Feta cheese

100g sun-dried tomatoes

1 small fresh bunch parsley, chopped

Serves 6–8

What you do

1 First, preheat your oven to 200°C/Fan 180°C/Gas 6. Prick the sweet potatoes all over with a fork, place in the oven on a baking tray and bake for about 45–60 minutes depending on their size, until soft right through.

2 Remove from the oven and leave to cool slightly, then halve and scoop out the soft potato into a mixing bowl. Add the grated onion and garlic and mix together.

3 Heat a small pan and toast the cumin and fennel seeds until aromatic, then add to the sweet potato with the paprika, black pepper, sea salt, plain flour, bulgar wheat, mozzarella, sun-dried tomatoes and parsley. Mix well to combine everything thoroughly.

Brush a 12"/30cm round cake tin (or use a rectangular roasting tin) with sunflower oil and line the base with parchment paper. Spoon half of the mixture in and press into place. Crumble the feta cheese over and then top with the remaining mixture, creating a sandwich effect.

4 Cut through into 8-12 portions and make a small hole about ¼ inch/¾ cm in the centre of the kibbeh. Drizzle with olive oil and bake for 1 hour, then remove and leave to cool a little before serving.

I serve the kibbeh at room temperature with a little salad garnish (try the Lebanese cabbage salad, page 66).

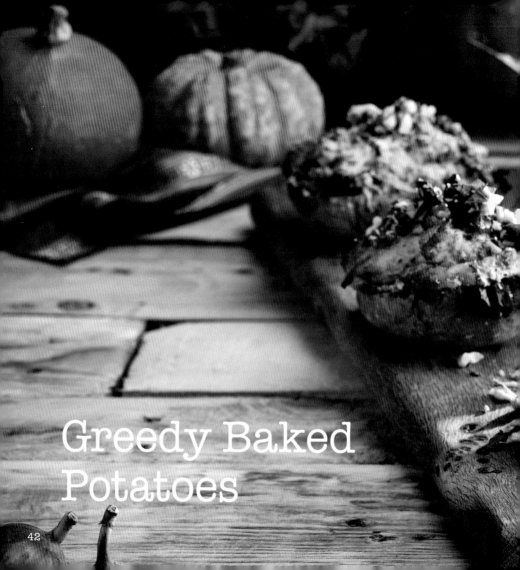

Greedy Baked Potatoes

Ingredients

3 large baking potatoes (the third potato is to create extra mash for the 4 halves)

1 large red onion

Filling

70g salted butter

3 tablespoons crème fraîche

60g blue cheese e.g. Perl Las or Roquefort

1 level teaspoon sea salt

¼ teaspoon ground white pepper

1 small leek, trimmed and shredded

200g spinach

To finish

25g walnuts

5 stems flat-leaf parsley leaves, chopped

1 tablespoon sultanas or dried cranberries

Serves 4

What you do

1 Heat the oven to 220°C/Fan 200°C/Gas 7. Bake the potatoes and the onion for about an hour or so, until soft all the way through. Cut the potatoes in half lengthways, scoop out the flesh into a ricer and pass into a bowl; keep the skins. Add 25g of the butter, the crème fraîche, Perl Las, salt and pepper into the potatoes. Fold in and combine well.

2 Peel the onion and chop finely, pop into a bowl and set aside.

3 Put 4 of the potato skins on an oven tray, divide 10g of the remaining butter between them and sprinkle with sea salt. Bake for 5–10 minutes until they crisp up, then remove from the oven.

4 Bring a saucepan half-filled with salted water to a boil, cook the shredded leek for 5 minutes, add the spinach and cook for a further 30 seconds. Drain, refresh under cold water and drain again. Squeeze out

as much water as you can, then fold into the mash.

5 Pile into the empty potato skins, then return them to the oven for 15 minutes more, until the top of the mash is crisp and browned.

6 Melt the remaining butter in a small frying pan on a high heat for 1 to 2 minutes, until it starts to brown, then fry the chopped walnuts for 30 seconds and stir in the chopped onion and sultanas.

7 Cook for 1 minute then stir in the parsley. Spoon over the potatoes and serve hot.

I really love a good baked spud with crisp skin and light, fluffy potato oozing with butter! I have brought together some of my favourite ingredients to create the ultimate greedily-filled jacket that is almost a complete meal in itself – perhaps a portion of cabbage salad and a dollop of slow-cooked red onions would be welcomed plate fellows.

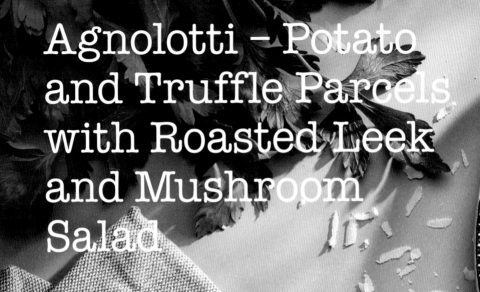

Agnolotti – Potato and Truffle Parcels with Roasted Leek and Mushroom Salad

Ingredients

Pasta dough

400g '00' pasta flour, plus extra for rolling out the pasta

½ teaspoon salt

3 large eggs, plus a little water if needed

Filling

225g prepared mashed potatoes (using a potato ricer gives best results)

75g mascarpone cheese

1 tablespoon truffle oil

Salt and freshly-ground black pepper

To serve

1 quantity of roasted mushroom and leek salad

1 tablespoon truffle oil

1 tablespoon Parmesan, grated

Serves 4

What you do

1 First, make the pasta dough for the agnolotti. Combine the flour and salt with your hand. Create a deep well in the middle of the flour and crack the eggs into it, whisking the eggs with a fork to combine.

2 As you whisk the eggs, begin gradually pulling in flour from the bottom and sides of the bowl. Once enough flour has been added, it will start forming a soft enough dough to roll out. You may need a little water to finish the dough and keep it soft.

3 Knead the dough on your work surface until it firms up and becomes smooth. Wrap in clingfilm and chill for 30 minutes.

4 Meanwhile, make the filling. Mix together the mashed potatoes, mascarpone and truffle oil, season well with sea salt and pepper and check the taste.

5 Roll out the pasta – unwrap the pasta, cut in half and run it through pasta rollers, starting at 0, and working through each number, finishing on 6. Pass it twice through each setting.

6 As the sheet of pasta comes off the pasta rollers, lay it on a floured work surface and cut into rectangular sheets about 28cm long. Sprinkle each sheet lightly with flour.

7 To assemble – fit a piping bag with a 1.5cm nozzle and spoon in the potato filling. Pipe a straight line of filling lengthwise along the pasta sheet, $\frac{1}{3}$ of the way in from the top edge; this will leave enough pasta at the top to fold over the filling. Moisten the edge with a little water and fold the pasta top over the filling and press firmly to seal. Then fold over again and trim along the bottom edge to neaten.

8 To make the agnolotti pockets, use the tips of your fingers to pinch the tube of pasta into equally-sized sections, creating little pillows and a seal between the pockets of filling. Use the pasta wheel or a sharp knife to separate the sections, cutting through each. You should be left with small individual pockets of filled pasta. Place the finished agnolotti on a tray of coarse polenta.

9 Repeat until all the pasta sheets and filling have been used. At this point the pasta can be cooked right away, covered and refrigerated overnight. You can also open freeze until solid on a large baking tray before transferring to containers or freezer bags. Bring a large pan of salted water to the boil, add the pasta bags and cook for 3 minutes or until tender. Drain well. Serve with a drizzle of truffle oil and a sprinkle of Parmesan and chopped parsley, or the lovely roasted leek and mushroom salad (page 50).

Roasted Leek and Mushroom Salad

Ingredients

4 large chestnut mushrooms, sliced super thin

1 large leek, trimmed, cut into 3 sections, then each section cut in half and shredded lengthways

2 tablespoons olive oil

1 flat teaspoon sea salt

1 teaspoon lemon zest, grated

1 tablespoon lemon juice

200g spinach

1 tablespoon parsley, chopped

Serves 4

What you do

1 Line 2 baking sheets with parchment paper.

2 Put the mushrooms and leeks in a large bowl and mix with the olive oil, salt, pepper, lemon zest and lemon juice.

3 Spread over the 2 baking sheets and place in the oven at 200°C/Fan 180°C/Gas 6.

4 Roast for 12 minutes then stir through and spread the leeks and mushrooms out to promote even cooking. Roast for a further 5–10 minutes until the tips of the leeks are slightly browned – this will intensify the flavour.

5 Remove and add half the spinach to each baking sheet, mix in and return to the oven, cooking for 5 minutes. Remove and stir in the chopped parsley.

6 To serve, divide the salad between 4 warmed bowls, reserving a little to garnish the agnolotti. Spoon the agnolotti on top of the salad and add a tablespoon of the pasta cooking water over the top of each serving. Finish with a drizzle of truffle oil, a good sprinkle of Parmesan and parsley.

Pappardelle with Game Ragu and Pangrattato

Game is in season at this time
of year and brings a welcomed
richness to recipes. This ragu is
a great introduction to cooking
game and appreciating the
complexity it can bring to a dish.
I also love serving this with
gnocchi and creamed polenta.

Ingredients

1 quantity pasta dough (see page 48), or use dried papardelle

1 teaspoon sea salt

Game ragu

Olive oil

1 small onion, peeled and very finely chopped

½ celery stalk, finely chopped

1 small carrot, peeled and very finely chopped

1 tablespoon chopped parsley

2 rabbit portions, duck legs, or pheasant weighing about 700g (you can mix the game) – all off the bone and chopped

1 chicken liver, chopped (optional)

500ml chicken or vegetable stock

1 Italian pork sausage, skinned and cut into pieces

75g minced pork

125ml red wine

125ml passata

1 bay leaf

2 juniper berries

To serve

Pangrattato

2 tablespoons olive oil

150g fresh white breadcrumbs – I like focaccia or ciabatta

6 stems flat-leaf parsley, leaves chopped

2 teaspoons unwaxed lemon zest

2 tablespoons Parmesan to finish

Serves 4

What you do

1 Heat a tablespoon of olive oil in a pan and add the onion, celery, and carrot, slowly sauté until the vegetables are light golden and slightly softened. I usually add a little water or stock during the frying process to help create steam, so that the vegetables cook quickly and evenly. Remove into a chef pan using a slotted spoon. Stir in the parsley.

② Next, cook the meats. Heat another tablespoon of olive oil and cook the sausage and minced pork until lightly browned. Remove with a slotted spoon and add to the chef pan. Then add the game, season with salt and pepper and lightly brown, adding the chopped chicken liver in at the end, add to the chef pan.

③ Add ⅓ of the wine to deglaze the pan, scraping up any caramelised meat juices, and pour over the vegetables and meat. Pour in the wine and cook for 1 minute to cook off the alcohol. Add the stock, passata, bay and juniper berries, bring to the boil then reduce the heat and simmer gently for about 1 hour until the game is soft. Meanwhile, make the pangrattato and the pappardelle. Heat the olive oil in a medium frying pan, stir in the breadcrumbs and gently fry until golden brown. Add the parsley, lemon zest, salt and pepper – set aside.

④ If making fresh papadelle, roll out the pasta into 4 long sheets, placing each one on a floured surface. Flour each, one at a time, and roll up into even index finger-thick slices. Quickly unravel and place either on a pasta drying tree or on a well-floured tray, but not in a clump!

⑤ When the ragu is ready, bring a large pan of water to the boil, add the salt and then the pappardelle. Cook for 3–4 minutes until al dente, then drain well. If using dried pasta, follow the instructions on the packet.

⑥ The finished ragu – the result should be a thickened meaty mass. If the sauce is a little watery, spoon out the meat and vegetables into a warm bowl and cook until the liquid is reduced.

⑦ When the ragu is ready, add it to the pappardelle, cooking for 5 minutes so it soaks up some of the sauce. Serve on warmed plates and top with the pangrattato and Parmesan.

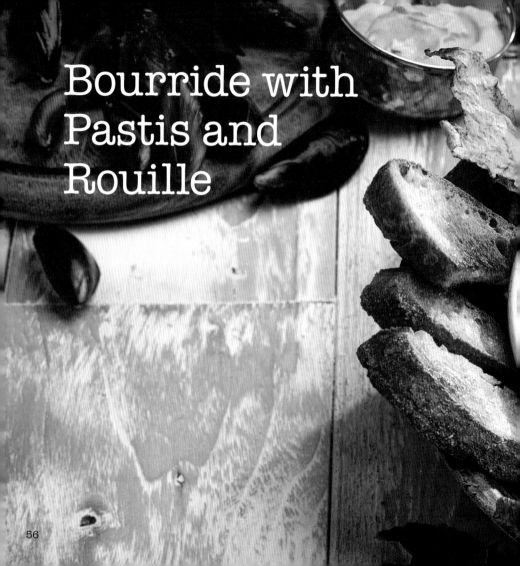

Bourride with Pastis and Rouille

Ingredients

The base

950ml fish stock – use the heads and shells of the prawns, white fish bones, add 1L of water and boil for 20 minutes with the carrot and leek trimmings. Season with salt and pepper to taste

60ml olive oil

1 teaspoon fennel seeds

2 medium onions, finely chopped

3 medium carrots, cut into thin slices

3 medium potatoes, cut into 8's

1 bay leaf

200g tinned cherry tomatoes

2 large garlic cloves, crushed

1 medium leek, trimmed and chopped

350ml dry white wine

The rest

1.2kg skinless firm white fish, such as cod, roll mops of sole, halibut or monkfish, in 6 good-sized chunks

12 medium prawns, peeled and deveined, tails removed

1–2 tablespoons pastis

½ teaspoon saffron threads, soaked in a little boiled water

Sea salt and freshly ground black pepper, to taste

To serve

2 tablespoons parsley, chopped

1 small baguette, sliced and toasted for serving

Serves 4

What you do

1 Heat the oil in a large chef or sauté pan over medium heat. Add the fennel seeds and lightly toast for 20 seconds, then add the onions, carrot, potato and bay leaf. Stir through, add a ladle of stock, pop a cartouche (parchment paper or foil sheet directly on top of the vegetables) and cook until soft, about 15 minutes.

2 Next, stir in the garlic and tomatoes and cook for 1 minute. Replace the cartouche and cook for a further 5 minutes; add a little more stock if the pan is dry. Remove the cartouche, add the leeks, stir and follow with the wine, then simmer for 5 minutes.

3 Add the remaining stock, saffron and pastis and season to taste with sea salt and pepper. Add enough water just to cover the vegetables and bring to the boil. Reduce the heat to medium-low and simmer gently until the broth is slightly reduced, about 12–15 minutes.

4 Add the fish pieces (do not stir after this otherwise they will break up). Place the cartouche back on top of the fish or add a lid so that the fish poaches and steams at the same time. Cook for 5 minutes then add the prawns. Cover and cook for a further 3 minutes.

5 Remove from the heat and finish with chopped parsley. Serve with toasted sliced baguette and rouille (see page 60).

Rouille

Ingredients

1 large garlic clove, grated

½ large red pepper, roasted, peeled and seeded

1 medium egg yolk

1 teaspoon freshly squeezed lemon juice

Small pinch saffron threads

200ml extra virgin olive oil

Sea salt

Serves 4

What you do

1 Combine the garlic, red pepper, egg yolk, lemon juice and saffron in a food processor.

2 Pulse until smooth, then slowly drizzle in the oil and process continuously until the mixture thickens.

3 Season with salt and pepper and use immediately.

Fish is generally not considered to be a comfort food, however, this recipe has so much depth of flavour and warms to the core. It reminds me of my time in the south of France, the end of the summer and feeling the seasons changing with cooler evenings. This has always been a welcomed bowl full of goodness with a little kick of pastis and is really delicious served with a classic rouille and baguette toasts.

Slow-Cooked Lamb with Red Wine, Orange and Green Olives

Ingredients

1kg chump Welsh lamb, cut into bite-size pieces

1 level teaspoon sea salt

¼ teaspoon black pepper

1 tablespoon olive oil

1 teaspoon butter

1 large onion, peeled and quartered

2 large carrots, peeled and cut into bite-size pieces

4 sticks celery, peeled with a vegetable peeler and cut into bite-size pieces

1 large orange, zest cut into strips with a vegetable peeler, juice kept

1 tablespoon sugar

6 garlic cloves, peeled and crushed

1 sprig each of thyme, bay and sage

400ml red wine

2 medium potatoes, peeled and each cut into 6 pieces

240g fat green olives

750ml–1L chicken or lamb stock

1 medium leek, cut into rounds

1 tablespoon cornflour or arrowroot to thicken

Gremolata to finish

2 rounded tablespoons parsley, chopped

1 teaspoon lemon zest, grated

½ teaspoon orange zest, grated

1 fat garlic clove, peeled and finely chopped

Serves 4

What you do

1 Mix the sea salt and black pepper together and rub over the lamb. Heat the olive oil and butter in a large frying pan, brown the lamb in batches and place in a large casserole dish.

2 Add the onion, carrots and celery to the frying pan (add a little more butter if needed) and cook them for about 5 minutes over

a medium heat until glossy and slightly browned at the edges. Add to the casserole pan.

3 Next, deglaze the pan with 100ml of the wine, scrape up any juices and pour into the casserole.

4 Wipe the pan out, place back on the heat, sprinkle in the sugar and add the strips of orange. Cook together until the sugar turns to a caramel, add the orange juice to loosen it and stir into the casserole. Add the garlic and herbs and mix though, then pour in the remaining red wine. Boil for 1 minute then pour into the casserole.

5 Add the potatoes and olives and enough stock just to cover the ingredients. Bring the casserole to the boil and then reduce the heat to a gentle simmer. Cover and cook for approximately 1½ hours, add the leeks and cook for a further 10 minutes. The meat should be beautifully tender.

6 Spoon the solid ingredients into a warmed serving dish with a slotted spoon. Thicken the juices with a little cornflour or arrowroot dissolved with a little water. Once thickened, pour over the lamb.

7 Mix everything together for the gremolata. Spoon the lamb into warmed bowls, sprinkle with the gremolata and serve.

I love Welsh lamb at this time of year, it has such a great flavour, having benefited from grazing on diverse summer pastures that include wild herbs.
It's world class.

Lebanese Cabbage Salad

This dish is inspired by the salad served at nearly every restaurant I visited when working in Ohrid, Macedonia. The local market had stalls there which would be piled high with cabbages and the people and restaurateurs knew exactly how to make the most of them. Our guests were always surprised by just how good they were.

Ingredients

1 medium cabbage, leaves washed, ribs removed, rolled and finely shredded

1 large garlic clove, grated

2 tablespoons dried mint or 4 tablespoons fresh mint, chopped

1 teaspoon sea salt

To finish

30ml olive oil

3-4 tablespoons lemon juice

Serves 6

What you do

1 Mix all the ingredients together; cover and leave to rest for 15 minutes to allow the flavours to mingle and the cabbage to slightly wilt.

2 Just before serving, add the lemon juice and olive oil and mix well.

3 Taste and add more lemon juice and salt as needed.

Note – I sometimes add a tablespoon of toasted sesame seeds, a teaspoon each of fennel and nigella seeds and 1 small, fresh, finely-chopped chilli.

We often serve this
as part of a lunch
to accompany roast
meats or fish at the
Cookery School.

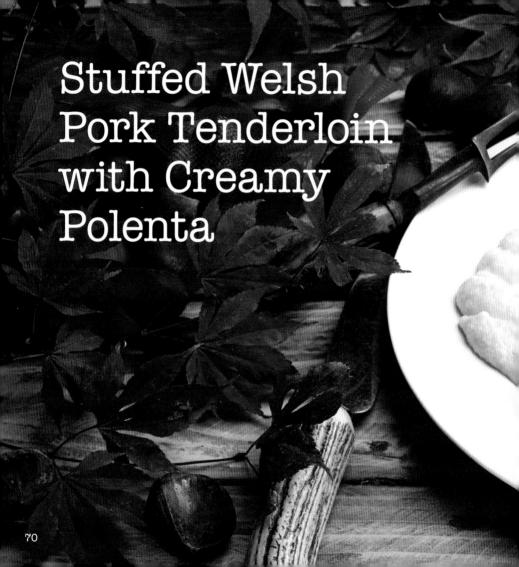

Stuffed Welsh Pork Tenderloin with Creamy Polenta

Ingredients

1 pork fillet, about 500g

Stuffing

1 medium onion, finely chopped

1 tablespoon olive oil

15g butter

150g pancetta or smoked bacon

2 fat garlic cloves, finely grated to a paste

¼ teaspoon freshly grated nutmeg

12 sage leaves

15 chestnuts, chopped

1 heaped tablespoon breadcrumbs

Sea salt and pepper

15 soft prunes, de-stoned

225g cooked spinach

6 slices cured ham, Prosciutto, St Danielle etc.

150ml white wine

1 tablespoon each of redcurrant jelly and pomegranate molasses

2 tablespoons crème fraîche

What you do

① First, prepare the stuffing, heat the olive oil/butter and add the onions and pancetta, cooking until lightly golden. Add a little of the white wine to deglaze any meat residue in the pan. Stir in the garlic, nutmeg, sage and chestnuts.

② Season with salt and pepper. Remove from the heat and stir in the breadcrumbs.

③ Prepare the tenderloin by removing any sinew with a sharp knife.

④ Cut almost right through and open out – 'butterfly'. Season the meat, lay the spinach on top and lightly season. Spoon the stuffing along the centre and pack down with your hands. Stud with the prunes.

⑤ Next, take a sheet of clingfilm

and brush with olive oil. Lay the slices of Parma ham overlapping along the clingfilm, place the pork on top and use the edge of the clingfilm to roll up like a Swiss roll. Tuck the edges in.

6 Weigh the fillet; it will need 15 minutes per 400g at 180°C/Fan 160°C/Gas 4.

7 Place the fillet in a baking tin lined with parchment paper, removing the cling film. Try to ensure the fillet is seal-side down.

8 Roast for the appropriate time, removing 5 minutes before the cooking time is complete. Brush with the redcurrant jelly and pomegranate molasses (mixed) and return to the oven for 5 minutes.

9 Remove from the oven, drain off the juices into a small saucepan, cover the meat and rest while you make the sauce. Add the remaining wine to the meat juices and boil rapidly to cook off the alcohol.

Stir in the crème fraîche, whisk and reduce the heat.

10 When the meat has rested for 15 minutes, cut into about 12 slices – add any juices that have escaped to the sauce.

This dish is delicious accompanied by creamy polenta, some steamed greens, such as cavolo nero, and some steamed carrots.

Creamy Polenta

Ingredients

500ml whole milk

1 bay leaf

3 sprigs thyme

1 large garlic clove, sliced

¼ teaspoon nutmeg, grated

250g instant polenta

75g Parmesan, grated

50g butter

Serves 4

What you do

1 Pour the milk into a pan and add 500ml of water. Add the bay leaf, thyme, garlic and nutmeg and bring to the boil. Turn off the heat and leave to infuse for 20 minutes.

2 Use a slotted spoon to remove the bay leaf, garlic and thyme, place back on the heat and return to the boil. Add the polenta in a steady stream, whisking steadily.

3 Cook for 1 minute until thickened. Simmer for 3 minutes, stirring all the time and then stir in the butter and Parmesan. Serve immediately.

Note – You can prepare this in advance up to the infused milk stage. Cool, cover and keep in the fridge until needed, then pick up the recipe from there.

This recipe is deliciously creamy and goes beautifully with roast meats and pan-fried fish. I use it as a quick alternative to mash potato and it equals it in terms of comfort.

Carrot and Cumin Salad

I often like a zesty mixed salad with a little protein, such as chunks of fish or feta, as a quick lunch or supper on a busy day. This salad really invigorates the palate.

Ingredients

500g organic carrots

1 teaspoon cumin seeds

1 teaspoon sea salt

3 large oranges

2 teaspoons orange flower water

4 teaspoons caster sugar or agave syrup

5 tablespoons lemon juice

Fresh ground cinnamon to sprinkle

To finish

6 stems mint leaves or parsley, chopped

Serves 6

What you do

1 Peel the carrots and coarsely grate, place in a large mixing bowl and sprinkle with the cumin seeds and sea salt. Mix well, cover and chill for 30 minutes.

2 Peel the oranges and cut the flesh into small pieces, catching and reserving any of the juices.

3 Mix the oranges with the orange flower water and sugar, cover and chill for 30 minutes.

4 To assemble, drain the carrots, squeeze in a tea towel and place back into the mixing bowl. Add the chilled oranges and juice, stir through and then add the lemon juice and cinnamon.

5 Spoon onto a serving dish and finish with chopped parsley or mint.

6 Keep chilled until ready to serve.

Autumn may not conjure up thoughts of salads, but this is vibrant, gorgeously colourful and fragrant, with a delicious combination of spice and citrus. Serve as part of a mezze or with rich roasted meats and grilled fish.

Roman-Style Chicken

Ingredients

1 large free-range chicken weighing about 2kg

2 tablespoons olive oil

The rub

1 teaspoon fennel seeds

1 teaspoon dried rosemary

1 teaspoon garlic granules

1 teaspoon lemon zest

1 flat teaspoon sea salt

$\frac{1}{4}$ teaspoon black pepper

Roasting glaze

50g butter

1 pinch saffron

1 tablespoon honey

2 tablespoons lemon juice

Fruit

4 fat fresh figs

400g black grapes

8 bay leaves

4 sprigs rosemary

Serves 4

What you do

1 Prepare the chicken – pat the chicken dry with a sheet of kitchen paper and coat with the olive oil. Place the rub ingredients in a pestle and mortar and pound together, tip onto your preparation board and then cover the chicken with the mixture. Make the roasting glaze by melting the butter, then adding the saffron, honey and lemon juice. When combined, paint all over the chicken.

2 Heat your oven to 200°C/Fan 180°C/Gas 6. Roast for 20 minutes to lightly brown the skin, then baste the chicken and reduce the temperature to 160°C/Fan 140°C/Gas 2 and continue roasting for 1 hour, basting every 20 minutes.

3 After 40 minutes, add the figs, grapes and rosemary sprigs and baste with the juices. Continue cooking until the hour is up.

④ Using a digital meat thermometer, check to see if the meat is cooked through. Insert into the thick part of the breast and then the thigh; you are looking for an internal temperature of 75°C.

⑤ Remove from the oven, cover and rest for 20 minutes before carving.

⑥ Remove the fruits and keep warm with the chicken. Deglaze the roasting pan with 200ml of medium-dry white wine, scraping up all the caramelised cooking juices. Taste and season accordingly. Also add in any juices that escape during carving. Pour into a warm jug and serve with the chicken and fruit.

I sometimes cook this recipe on the BBQ to give it a lovely light, smoky flavour. So good!

Shakshuka

This is one of my quick-fix dishes that 'hits the mark'. It's especially lovely served on a chilly late autumn morning as a brunch dish.

Ingredients

2 tablespoons olive oil

25g butter

2 small onions, peeled and thinly sliced

1 red or green pepper, halved, deseeded and sliced

1–2 red chillies, deseeded and sliced

2 garlic cloves, pasted with a little sea salt

400g can chopped tomatoes

1 teaspoon caster sugar

8 free-range eggs

Small bunch parsley, coriander and mint, roughly chopped

4 dessertspoons thick, creamy yogurt

Serves 4

What you do

1 Heat the oil in a heavy-based frying pan and add the butter. Stir in the onions and peppers and cook until soft – add a little water to speed this up. Make sure the onions are super soft and slightly golden.

2 Add the chilli and garlic, cook for 1 minute, then stir in the tomatoes and sugar, mixing well. Cook over a medium-low heat until the liquid has reduced and thickened slightly, then season with a little sea salt and pepper.

3 Using a wooden spoon, create 6 pockets in the tomato mixture and crack an egg into each. Cover the pan and cook the eggs over a low heat until the whites are cooked and the yolks soft – about 5 minutes.

4 Beat the yogurt lightly then spoon in between the eggs and top with the chopped herbs. Serve with crusty bread – delish!

I often make shakshuka on
my day off when I share a
lovely brunch with Mr. Gray.
I sometimes add leftover sliced
potatoes in with the onion and
peppers, making it a more
substantial dish.

Beef in Ale
with Yorkshire
Pudding

Ingredients

4 tablespoons olive oil

1.5kg Welsh chuck steak, cut into bite-size pieces

450g button onions or shallots, peeled and left whole

3 fat garlic cloves, grated

2 tablespoons demerara sugar

350g portobello mushrooms, thickly sliced

2 tablespoons plain flour

2 teaspoons English mustard powder

450ml Belgian-style dark ale or a good British equivalent

3 sprigs fresh thyme

2 bay leaves

Yorkshire Pudding

250g plain white flour

Pinch of salt

150ml whole milk

150ml cold water

5 free-range eggs, beaten

2 tablespoons beef dripping or sunflower oil

Serves 6

What you do

1 Preheat the oven to 150°C/Fan 130°C/Gas 2. Heat half the olive oil in a large ovenproof casserole until hot (test for readiness with a cube of meat). Brown the meat all over in small batches, adding the remaining oil if needed. Transfer each batch to a plate while you continue cooking the rest of the meat.

2 Add the onions to the pan and cook over a medium heat, stirring occasionally for 5 minutes or until they start to soften and colour. Add the garlic and sugar; fry for 4–5 minutes or until the onions are soft and caramelised for full flavour. Add the mushrooms and cook for 2–3 minutes, then turn the heat down and return the meat and any juices to the casserole.

3 Stir in the flour, mustard and

plenty of seasoning and mix in with a wooden spoon. Gradually pour in the beer, stirring as you go. Slowly bring to a gentle simmer, add the thyme, bay leaves and cover with a lid.

④ Place the casserole in the oven and cook for 3–3½ hours. The beef should be tender and the sauce dark and rich.

⑤ Whilst the beef is cooking, make the Yorkshire pudding batter.

⑥ Sift the flour into a large bowl with a generous pinch of salt. Combine the milk in a jug with 150ml cold water.

⑦ Make a well in the middle of the flour and add the eggs. Pour in a little milk and water and then whisk the lot together to make a smooth batter. Mix in the rest of the liquid until you have a batter which is the consistency of single cream. Cover and leave at room temperature until the beef is cooked.

⑧ Once the casserole has come out of the oven, turn the temperature up to 220°C/Fan 200°C/Gas 7. Place a large roasting tin or a 12-hole muffin tin, greased liberally with dripping or oil, on a high shelf and leave for 10 minutes to get hot. Meanwhile, check the flavour of the casserole and adjust the seasoning accordingly. Place the lid back on and keep warm.

⑨ Carefully take the tin out of the oven and keep warm on the hob if possible whilst you ladle in the batter. Put the puddings into the oven and cook for 15–20 minutes until well-risen and golden. Keep an eye on them towards the end of the cooking time, but do not be tempted to open the door until they are beautifully bronzed, because they will deflate!

⑩ Serve the Yorkshire puddings on warmed plates and fill with the beef and sauce.

Note – I like to add a simple vegetable to serve with this, steamed greens or carrots are perfect.

Linguine with Crab and Chilli

Crab meat and chilli are a match made in heaven, perfect for running through linguini, tagliatelle and spaghetti. Delish!

Ingredients

400g dried linguine/spaghetti or use fresh pasta for 4 servings

50ml extra virgin olive oil

1 large garlic clove, peeled and grated

2 tablespoons chopped tinned cherry tomatoes

1 anchovy, super finely chopped

¼ teaspoon dried chilli flakes

300g fresh white crab meat

1 tablespoon fresh parsley, finely chopped

1½ tablespoons lemon juice

To finish

2 tablespoons fried breadcrumbs

1 tablespoon fresh parsley, chopped

To finish

2 tablespoons fried breadcrumbs

1 tablespoon fresh parsley, chopped

Serves 4

What you do

1 If making the pasta by hand, roll out the pasta dough using a pasta machine working from 0 through to 7, running the sheets twice through each setting. Cut into 4 long sheets as explained on page 48, placing each one on a floured surface. Pass through the linguine setting on your pasta machine, or flour each sheet one at a time, roll up into a fat cigar shape and cut into thin, even slices. Quickly unravel and place either on a pasta drying tree or a well-floured tray, but not in a clump together!

2 Cook the pasta in a large pan of boiling salted water for 8–12 minutes if using packet pasta (check instructions on the pack), or 3–4 minutes if fresh, until al dente.

3 Meanwhile, make the sauce – put the olive oil and garlic in a saucepan and fry for 1 minute, add the tomato, anchovy and chilli flakes followed by the crab meat, parsley

and lemon juice and sauté for 5 minutes over a medium heat.

4 Drain the pasta, return to the pan, add the crab sauce and briefly toss together. Season to taste. Divide among 4 warmed plates and finish with the breadcrumbs and parsley, serving immediately.

Fresh crab is perfect in this pasta recipe, it has such a natural sweetness which really marries well with chilli and citrus. You can also try the recipe using cockles and queenie scallops for a change.

Lahmacun

Ingredients

The dough

400g bread flour, plus extra to dust

3 tablespoons dried milk powder

2 teaspoons sea salt

3 teaspoons fast-action dried yeast

2 teaspoons caster sugar

100ml olive oil

1 large egg

120ml lukewarm water

Extra olive oil to knead the dough/
oil the bowl

Topping

300g good-quality minced Welsh lamb

1 medium onion, finely chopped

1½ teaspoons sea salt

2 teaspoons ground cinnamon

2 teaspoons ground allspice

1 teaspoon red chilli flakes

5 stems flat-leaf parsley, leaves chopped

2 tablespoons pomegranate molasses

2 dessertspoons sumac

To assemble and serve

3–4 tablespoons tahini

30g pine nuts

2 tablespoons lemon juice

4 tablespoons Greek yoghurt

8 pickled chillies

Chopped parsley

Serves 4

What you do

1 First, make the dough – put the flour, milk powder, salt, yeast and sugar in a large mixing bowl and stir well to combine. Make a well in the centre and pour in the oil, break in the egg and mix both together briefly to combine. Pour in the water and mix through the dry ingredients to form a soft dough ball. If it is a little wet, add some flour to firm it up.

2 Wash your hands and knead the dough lightly for about 5 minutes on an oiled surface to form a smooth ball. Place in an oiled bowl, brush the surface of the dough with olive oil, cover and leave in a warm place until doubled in size, about an hour.

3 To make the topping – put the beef, onion, sea salt, cinnamon, allspice, chilli, parsley, pomegranate molasses and sumac in a mixing bowl and mix thoroughly with your hands. Cover and place in the fridge until needed.

4 Divide the risen dough into 2 equal portions for large, or into 8 equal portions for individual bases. Roll each into a thin base, dinner plate-size for large, saucer-size for small. Brush each lightly with olive oil on both sides and place on the baking sheets. Cover and leave to rise slightly, about 15 minutes.

5 Preheat your oven to 210°C/Fan 190°C/Gas 7.

6 To assemble – divide the tahini between the bases, then divide the topping and spread it evenly. Finish with a scatter of pine nuts and a gentle squeeze of lemon juice.

7 Bake in the oven for 15 minutes; the crust should be lightly golden at the edges. Remove and finish the top with blobs of yoghurt, arrange a few pickled chillies and scatter some fresh chopped parsley. Serve with a lovely salad – I like to spoon a mound of it on top!

This is a delicious Turkish/Byzantine style flatbread topped with ground Welsh lamb. You can also use ground beef or keep it vegetarian using finely chopped vegetables such as onion, grated squash and aubergine.

Harvest Curry Supper

I love a curry night and this one celebrates the beginning of autumn, when there are so many veggies to choose from. I often change the ones I use depending on what I have. Beetroot, carrot and sweet potato work well as a combo. Pre-roasting the vegetables adds a good depth of flavour and character to the finished dish.

Ingredients

Curry

Sunflower oil for frying

1 large aubergine, cut into bite-size pieces

1 medium cauliflower, cut into bite-size pieces

300g butternut squash, peeled and cubed

2 medium onions, peeled and thinly sliced

1 walnut-size piece ginger, peeled with a teaspoon and finely chopped

4 large garlic cloves, peeled and finely grated to a paste

3 green 'finger' chillies, chopped

1 teaspoon turmeric

2 tablespoons fresh ground spice mix (see next column)

500g chopped tinned tomatoes

300ml vegetable stock (I use Swiss Marigold Vegetable Powder)

200ml coconut cream

2 stems curry leaves to finish

Spice mix

2 teaspoons coriander seeds

1 teaspoon cumin seeds

1 star anise

1 cinnamon stick

3 cloves

2 green cardamom pods

½ teaspoon black peppercorns

1 teaspoon fennel seeds

½ teaspoon fenugreek

To finish

1 tablespoon lemon juice

Serves 6

What you do

1 Place the aubergine, cauliflower and squash in a large roasting tin lined with parchment, drizzle with oil, mix through and season with sea salt and black pepper. Roast in the oven at 200°C/Fan 180°C/Gas 6 for about 30 minutes until soft

and lightly golden in colour. You will need to turn the vegetables halfway through the cooking time so that they roast evenly.

② Meanwhile, prepare the base of the curry. Roast the spice mix in a heated pan until aromatic. Place in a spice or coffee grinder and whiz to a powder.

③ Next, start the curry. Heat 3 tablespoons of sunflower oil in a large pan, add the onion, stir through, add 2 tablespoons of water, cover with a lid and sauté until soft and just turning lightly golden. Add the garlic, chilli and ginger, stir through and cook for about 3 minutes until the raw aroma subsides. Tip in the roasted vegetables, tinned tomatoes and stock. Bring to the boil and then reduce the heat and simmer for 30 minutes until the sauce has thickened. Stir in the coconut cream and season to taste – I like to add a squeeze of lemon juice to brighten the flavour.

④ Finish with the curry leaves and serve with poori bread (see page 104) or rice and the vada cakes (see page 105).

I have added poori breads; naughty, but so good! The little split pea fritters add a delicious and complimentary flavour and texture to the dish. Enjoy!

Poori Breads

Ingredients

400g wholemeal flour (atta or chapati flour)

1½ level teaspoons sea salt

160–200ml warm water (adjust as you go)

Sunflower oil for deep frying

Serves 6–8

What you do

1 Mix the flour and salt in a bowl until well combined. Make a well in the centre, add ¾ of the warm water and roughly mix with the flour. Keep trickling in the water until you achieve a soft dough that you feel you could roll out without being too tough, or too sticky.

2 Place the dough on your worktop and knead until smooth, about 2 minutes. Once the dough is ready, leave it in a bowl and set aside, covered, for about 20 minutes.

3 Remove the dough from the bowl, knead again briefly and roll it into a longish log. Pinch off small golf ball-sized portions and roll out into smooth balls.

4 Generously dust your work surface with flour and roll into circles of about 0.5cm thickness. Lay them on to a floured area without overlapping.

5 When you have just 3–4 pooris complete, heat the oil and bring it to a smoking point. Drop in a small piece of dough and check if it quickly sizzles and rises to the surface. That's your cue to get started on frying the pooris.

6 Very gently pick up the rolled poori, starting with the one you rolled first, and ease into the hot oil. Work with one poori at a time. Once you have a poori in the oil, use a slotted spoon or tongs and move the oil around so it cooks evenly.

7 Once it is puffed on one side, carefully turn over so both sides are cooked and have brown spots. Transfer to a baking sheet lined with kitchen paper to drain. Continue with the remaining pooris.

8 You can keep them warm in the oven until ready to serve.

Vada Cakes

Ingredients

480g Chana dal – yellow split peas

3-4 rounded tablespoons chickpea flour

1 large onion, peeled and very finely chopped

2-3 green chilies, finely chopped

2 teaspoons ginger, finely chopped

1 teaspoon fennel seeds

3 stems curry leaves, finely chopped

$\frac{1}{8}$ teaspoon asafoetida

Sea salt

500ml sunflower oil

Serves 6-8

What you do

1 Soak the dal in water for 3 hours and then drain.

2 To create a bind for the mixture, spoon $\frac{1}{3}$ of the dal into a food processor and process to a thick paste. Add the remaining dal and pulse to a course texture.

3 Tip the mixture into a bowl and stir in the chickpea flour to make a mixture that holds together when

squeezed. Before forming into little cakes, mix in the onion, chillies, ginger, fennel seeds, curry leaves, asafoetida and season with sea salt – taste to check.

4 Heat the oil in a heavy-bottomed wok or deep-sided frying pan (the oil should come ⅓ up the sides). When the oil is hot, wet the palms of your hands and shape about a tablespoon of the dal mixture into a 10cm round disc.

5 Slide the vada gently into the hot oil. Repeat with the remaining mix. Fry for approximately 3 to 5 minutes until they turn golden brown and crisp. Drain on kitchen paper and serve with the vegetable curry and a fruity chutney.

Mango, Tamarind and Ginger Chutney

Ingredients

80g seedless tamarind pulp

2 tablespoons sunflower oil

1 medium red onion, peeled and finely diced

1 piece cassia bark

3 green cardomom pods, cracked

1 star anise

1 bay leaf

½ teaspoon fresh red or green chilli, finely chopped

2 teaspoons grated ginger

1 dessertspoon garam masala

4 medium mangos, diced

8 tablespoons soft dark brown sugar

½ teaspoon sea salt

Makes about 600g

What you do

1 To make the tamarind juice, put the pulp in a bowl and cover with 125ml boiling water. Stir well and let soak for 10 to 15 minutes. Set a fine-meshed strainer over another bowl, add the soaked tamarind and press hard with a wooden spoon to extract the juice. This should give you around 250ml. Discard the solids left in the strainer.

2 To make the chutney, heat the oil in a pan, add the onion and cook until soft. Add the cassia bark, cardamom pods, star anise and bay leaf. Stir in the chilli, ginger and garam masala, cooking for 1 minute.

3 Add the mangoes and stir through. Add the brown sugar and salt and stir to dissolve, then add the tamarind. Simmer until the juices thicken – about 40 minutes. Spoon into sterilised jars and seal.

Baked Apples
with Caramel
Sauce

Ingredients

6 good-sized eating apples

Brushing

50g butter

50g molasses or soft brown sugar

1 tablespoon lemon juice

1 tablespoon orange juice

¼ teaspoon ground cinnamon

Filling

2 handfuls dried fruit (ready to eat apricots, prunes, raisins and cherries, chopped)

1 piece stem ginger in syrup, chopped

Zest of 1 orange

2 tablespoons brandy, rum or whisky

Topping

1 tablespoon of whole nuts e.g. pistachio, walnut or hazelnuts

12 amaretti biscuits

Serves 6

What you do

1 Preheat the oven to 180°C/Fan 160°C/Gas 4. Carefully remove the core from the apples with a sharp knife or apple corer. Slice each apple into 6 rings.

2 Melt the butter and sugar together for the brushing of the slices, add the lemon/orange juices and cinnamon and boil for 2 minutes.

3 Remove from the heat and brush each apple slice with the mixture, then reassemble the slices to form a whole apple and place them in a baking tin lined with parchment. Mix the ingredients together for the filling and press into the centre of each apple.

4 Bake the apples in the preheated oven for 30–40 minutes until really soft and gooey.

5 To finish – place the nuts and amaretti biscuits in a processor and blitz down to a fine crumb. Remove

the apples from the oven and spoon the crumb mixture over the top. Serve with créme fraîche or Greek yoghurt. I love a tablespoon of date molasses over everything as well.

I have been making baked apples since I was in school. They were always a popular dessert at home and my mum introduced using dark muscovado in the filling, which I love.

Autumn Fruit Pie

This is a bumper-size pie packed full of autumnal goodies, all wrapped up in a delicious, rich crust. It really makes a statement when presented to guests and there is always a slice left for next day's breakfast!

Ingredients

Cinnamon Pastry

500g all purpose flour

100g walnuts or slivered almonds, toasted and ground

4 tablespoons caster sugar

2 teaspoons ground cinnamon

1 teaspoon sea salt

1 teaspoon vanilla paste

200g chilled unsalted butter, cut into 1.5cm pieces

75g chilled solid vegetable shortening, cut into 1.5cm pieces

1 teaspoon orange zest, grated

1 medium egg, beaten

A little chilled water, if needed

Filling

2 tablespoons ground rice

600g (prepared weight) sliced Bramley apples

6 plums or 12 damsons, halved and stones removed

Juice of ½ an orange

12 soft, dried apricots, halved

2 tablespoons dried cranberries

6 dried pear halves, sliced

12 soft amaretti biscuits

1 rounded teaspoon ground cinnamon

1 teaspoon ground ginger

¼ teaspoon ground cloves

3 nuggets of stem ginger, sliced

3 tablespoons brandy

1 tablespoon cornflour

Finishing

1 medium egg beaten

2 tablespoons demerara sugar

Serves 12

What you do

1 To make the pastry – briefly blend the flour, nuts, sugar, cinnamon, sea salt and vanilla paste in a food processor. Add the chilled butter and vegetable shortening and pulse until the mixture looks

like coarse breadcrumbs. Add the orange zest and the beaten egg and pulse again. Remove the lid and press some of the mixture together – if it looks a little dry or cracks when pressed together, add a tablespoon of chilled water. You may need more or none at all depending on the moisture in the ingredients.

2 Tip the dough onto your work surface and form into a ball, then flatten and wrap in clingfilm. Refrigerate until just firm enough to roll out – about 30 minutes.

3 Make the filling by peeling, coring and slicing the apples thinly.

4 Place in a bowl, squeeze in the orange juice and then add all the other ingredients.

5 Butter and lightly flour a 30cm pizza or baking dish. Roll out $\frac{1}{3}$ of the dough on a floured work surface to approximately 34cm round and line the base, pressing it gently into place. The pastry will be larger than the base, but you will use this to form an edge for the lid.

6 Fold the edges of the pastry in so it forms a border all the way round. Brush with beaten egg, then sprinkle the ground rice over the pastry base. Pile in the filling and roll out the rest of the pastry to cover the top. Press the edges together and pinch using your index finger and thumb, creating a decorative finish. Cover and chill until cold – about 30 minutes.

7 Glaze the top with egg wash and sprinkle with demerara sugar.

8 Bake in a preheated oven at 180°C/Fan 160°C/Gas 4. Cook for 25 minutes then turn down the oven to 150°C/Fan 130°C/Gas 3 and cook for a further 20 minutes. The finished pie should be beautifully golden. Serve warm with whipped double cream, Greek yoghurt or crème fraîche.

Yummy Prune and Chocolate Clafoutis

This is one of my favourite desserts. I remember tasting it for the first time at La Bouteille d'Or, a lovely bistro I would visit occasionally when I worked in Paris. Following that experience I think I made every type of clafoutis possible and this combination only just beats my second favourite – cherries. You can make it in individual tins or little dishes, but it looks so good served in a large dish.

Ingredients

A little butter for brushing

Baking parchment paper for lining

12 large, juicy Agen prunes, stones removed, or soft ready to eat prunes

90g dark chocolate, cut into pieces

Batter

3 free-range eggs, separated

75g caster sugar

70g plain flour

1 teaspoon vanilla paste

150ml double cream

100ml whole milk

1 teaspoon brandy

¼ teaspoon sea salt

To finish

Icing sugar for dusting

Serves 6

What you do

1 Butter the inside of a dish large enough to fit the prunes in a single layer.

2 To make the batter – whisk the egg yolks with half the sugar until thickened and pale in colour.

3 Sift in the flour and whisk, followed by the vanilla paste, cream, milk, brandy and salt. In a separate bowl, whisk the egg whites with the remaining sugar until stiff and peaks are formed, but not dry. Gently fold into the batter with a large metal spoon. Pour the batter into the prepared dish and scatter in the chocolate pieces.

4 Preheat your oven to 220°C/Fan 200°C/Gas 7.

5 Bake for 10 minutes, then lower the oven temperature to 200°C/Fan 180°C/Gas 6 and bake for a further 10–15 minutes. Insert a skewer; it should come out clean when ready.

6 Leave to stand for 5 minutes before serving. Dust with icing sugar and serve.

Note – Soak the prunes in Armagnac, brandy or Port – place the prunes in a sterile jar, cover with your chosen tipple and leave in a cool place for 7 days. Use the prunes as instructed in the recipe and serve the alcoholic prune juice to drizzle over the portions.

Soak the prunes in Armagnac, brandy or Port – place the prunes in a sterile jar, cover with your chosen tipple and leave in a cool place for 7 days.

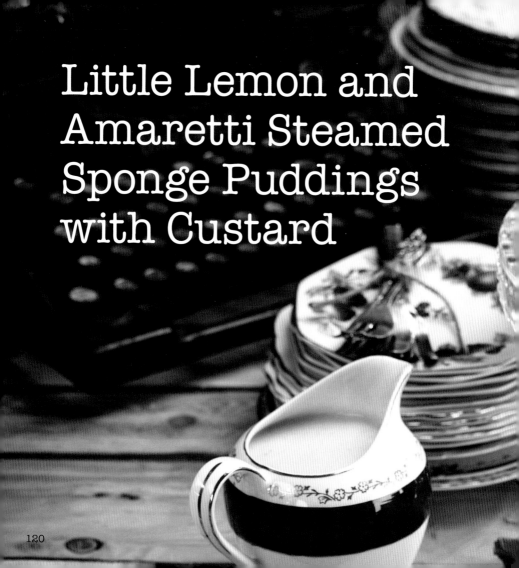

Little Lemon and Amaretti Steamed Sponge Puddings with Custard

Ingredients

Syrup

4 small lemons – these will be zested, reserve the juice for the syrup and the sponge

100g caster sugar

6 tablespoons lemon juice

60ml water

1 tablespoon Limoncello

The sponge

175g unsalted butter, softened

175g caster sugar

3 large free-range eggs

175g self-raising flour

2 tablespoons lemon juice

3 tablespoons whole milk

8 amaretti biscuits

Serves 8

What you do

1 First, make the syrup – thinly peel the zest from the lemons and cut them into super thin strips, 'julienne'. Take ⅓ and pop into a mixing bowl for the sponge, place the rest in a small saucepan and add the sugar, lemon juice and water. Bring to the boil and then simmer for 5 minutes until slightly thickened. Remove from the heat, stir in the Limoncello and set aside.

2 To make the sponge, lightly butter the inside of 8 pudding moulds or ramekins and line the base of each with a little square of baking paper (if you're cooking your puddings in ramekins or cups and don't plan to turn them out for serving, skip the baking paper). Set aside.

3 Cream the butter, sugar and lemon zest in the bowl of a stand mixer until light and fluffy or use an electric hand whisk. Add the eggs, one at a time, whisking well to mix after each addition. Sift in the flour, mix well and then add 4 tablespoons of the reserved lemon juice and gently mix until smooth.

4 Preheat your oven to 180°C/Fan 160°C/Gas 4. If you have a steam setting on your oven, set at 'full steam'. If you don't, you can use the bain-marie method by placing the puddings in a roasting tin and $\frac{1}{3}$ filling it with hot water.

5 To assemble – spoon the syrup between the moulds, top with the sponge mixture and insert an amaretti biscuit into each. Cover each with a piece of pleated foil and press around the moulds to seal, but not too tightly, as they need enough 'give' to rise a little.

6 Put the moulds onto a rack or perforated tray and steam for 25 minutes, or use the bain-marie method.

7 Stand for 5 minutes before turning out and serving with cream, ice cream or custard.

I love serving them on a cake stand like the one in the photograph. It creates a little theatre at the table and looks fabulous.

Custard

Ingredients

400ml whole milk

200ml double cream

1 teaspoon vanilla paste

6 medium egg yolks

2 tablespoons caster sugar

1 tablespoon cornflour

What you do

1 Pour the milk and cream into a heavy-bottomed pan with the vanilla and set over medium heat. Stir to mix the vanilla then bring to a very gentle simmer, but do not allow it to boil!

2 Meanwhile, beat together the yolks, sugar and cornflour in a large heat-proof bowl. Pour the hot milk onto the yolk and sugar mixture, whisking vigorously.

3 Turn the heat right down and pour the custard back into a clean, dry pan. Stirring continuously, heat until the custard thickens enough to coat the back of your wooden spoon – the longer you cook it, the thicker it will get. This does take a little time; keep going and don't stop stirring!

4 Pour into a warm jug and press clingfilm onto the surface to prevent a skin from forming.

I have to admit to always doubling the recipe when I make custard. I have discovered over the years when entertaining that other people love it too, and lots of it!

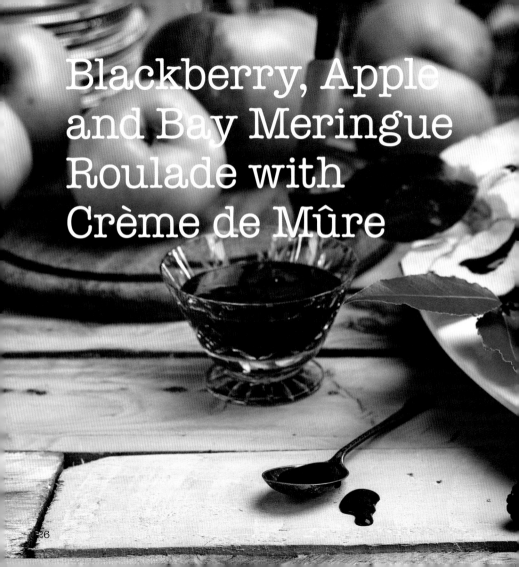

Blackberry, Apple and Bay Meringue Roulade with Crème de Mûre

Ingredients

Syrup

300g blackberries

1 teaspoon lemon juice

2 bay leaves

2–3 tablespoons sugar, to sweeten

4 tablespoons crème de mûre
(blackberry liqueur) or crème de
cassis (blackcurrant liqueur)

Apple Crisp Garnish

1 eating apple

50ml water

1 tablespoon caster sugar

Apple Purée

1 large Bramley apple, peeled, cored
and chopped

25g caster sugar

4 tablespoons water

The meringue

4 large egg whites

250g caster sugar

2 teaspoons vanilla essence

1 teaspoon white wine vinegar

1 teaspoon cornflour

Filling

400ml double cream

100ml thick Greek yoghurt

1 tablespoon icing sugar, plus a little
extra to dust

300g fresh blackberries

1 x apple purée recipe

To finish

12 blackberries

8 bay leaves

Serves 8

What you do

1 Set your oven at 200°C/Fan 180°C/Gas 6. Line the base and sides of a Swiss roll tin (33cm x 24cm) with a sheet of parchment paper. Tip the sugar onto the paper and spread out evenly. Place in the oven and cook until the sugar starts to melt at the edges (not caramelise), about 8 minutes.

2 Whisk the egg whites in a large clean bowl with an electric mixer until they begin to firm up. (I usually wipe the inside of the bowl with a slice of lemon, then dry with kitchen paper.) Add the hot caster sugar in a slow stream, whisking until you get a firm, glossy meringue. Use a large metal spoon to fold in the vanilla essence, vinegar and cornflour. Spread inside the lined tin and level with a palette knife.

3 Pop into the oven and lower the heat to 160°C/Fan 140°C/Gas 3. Bake for 30 minutes, until it is firm to the touch and crisp on top.

4 Make the apple crisps for the garnish – cut the apple into super-thin slices (a mandolin is perfect for this). Heat the water and sugar together and boil for 5 minutes. Add the apple slices and mix gently, cooking for 3 minutes. Remove and then place the slices onto a baking sheet lined with parchment paper. Pop them in the oven at the same time as the meringue and cook for about 30 minutes until slightly crisp; they will get crisper as they cool.

5 To make the apple purée, place the chopped apples in a pan with the sugar and water and bring to the boil. Reduce to a simmer and stir; the apples will begin to collapse and form the purée. Once you have a thick purée, spoon into a bowl and leave to cool.

6 Meanwhile, make the syrup – put the blackberries, lemon juice, bay leaves and 2 tablespoons of sugar (taste at the end to decide if you would like it sweeter) over a medium-high heat, stirring until the sugar has dissolved and the blackberries begin to give up their juice. Simmer for 5 minutes then tip into a sieve placed over a bowl. Push the juice and pulp through into the bowl, discarding the seeds and bay. Taste and add more sugar if needed. Stir in the crème de mûre or crème de cassis and leave to cool.

7 Once the meringue is cooked, gently tip out onto a piece of parchment paper and carefully peel away the paper from the base. Now it is ready to fill and roll up.

8 Make the filling – whisk the cream until thickened and silky smooth, add the icing sugar, the Greek yoghurt and fold in the apple purée. Take out 2 rounded tablespoons and reserve for the top. Crush the blackberries and ripple through the filling with 4 tablespoons of the syrup. Spread over the meringue, leaving a thin border around the edge. Roll up, pulling the edge of the parchment

nearest you upwards and forwards; keep going until the seam is underneath.

9 Carefully ease the roulade onto a serving plate. Dot or pipe the reserved cream along the centre and dot with apple crisps and blackberries, inserting the bay leaves in between. Dust with icing sugar and serve with the remaining syrup.

Preserves

Autumn Fruit
Chutney

Autumn Fruit Chutney

Ingredients

450g sherry or red wine vinegar

750g light muscovado sugar

1 tablespoon allspice

4 x star anise

2 sticks cinnamon

100g fresh ginger, grated

3 long red chillies, split

1kg plums, halved, stoned and cut into small pieces

750g pears, peeled, cored and cut into small pieces

250g grapes, cut in half – seeds removed

750g Bramley apples, peeled, cored and cut into small pieces

5 bay leaves

Makes 5 x 350ml jars, plus 1 small 150ml taster jar

What you do

1 Pour the sherry or red wine vinegar, the sugar, spices, cinnamon, ginger and chillies into a large pan and bring to the boil, stirring until the sugar melts. Boil for 5 minutes then add the fruit. Stir and bring up to the boil again and add the bay leaves.

2 Bring the pan to a simmer and cook the fruit for about 1 ½ hours, stirring from time to time to prevent sticking.

3 Sterilise your jars, ready to use. (See page 137.)

4 Spoon the hot chutney into the jars and seal straight away. Cool and then store in a cool, dark place. Leave to mature for a month before using.

Note – This is deliciously fruity and goes with so many things. I especially like it on top of hot bubbling Welsh rarebit!

133

Slow-Cooked Onions with Balsamic Vinegar

The slow-cooked onions in balsamic and the pickled damsons are two of my very favourite preserves. They go with just about everything and have even found their way onto my Sunday brunch plate, nestling next to the crispy bacon and bangers!

Ingredients

6 large red onions, peeled – you can use white onions if you don't have red

2 large red chillies, split and deseeded

3 garlic cloves, peeled and halved

3 sprigs rosemary

5 rounded tablespoons soft dark brown sugar

250ml balsamic, sherry or red wine vinegar

Makes approximately 500g

What you do

1 Line a roasting tin with parchment paper.

2 Cut the onions in half around the middle, trim the root and top end and arrange them in the tin. Place the chillies and garlic between the onions and tuck the rosemary in between them.

3 Mix together the sugar and balsamic vinegar, spoon over the onions and pour in the rest. Roast at 160°C/Fan 140°C/Gas 2 for approximately 2 hours or until the onions are soft, slightly caramelised on top and the juices thickened.

4 Spoon into a 500ml sterile jar or 2 x 250ml jars, seal and keep in the fridge.

Note – This delicious relish goes with just about everything, from breakfast bangers and cheese on toast to cold meats, a good sarnie and a cheese board.

To sterilise your jars, wash them thoroughly in hot soapy water, rinse well and drain on a clean tea towel. Preheat your oven to 120°C/Fan 100°C/Gas 2 for 5 minutes. Place the clean jars on the oven racks with space between them and heat for 10–15 minutes. Job done!

Pickled Damsons

I have always made it my
business to find out where there
is a supply of damsons, sloes,
rosehips and blackberries.

Ingredients

1kg damsons

1 small stick cinnamon

2 cloves

1 teaspoon allspice berries

1 walnut-size piece of ginger

The pared rind of half a medium unwaxed lemon

300ml balsamic vinegar

500g brown sugar

Makes approximately 1.5kg

What you do

1 Wash the damsons and remove the stalks.

2 Tie the spices, ginger and lemon peel in a small piece of muslin.

3 Put the spices in a non-reactive saucepan with the vinegar and sugar. Stir over medium heat until the sugar has dissolved. Add the fruit and simmer until tender but not disintegrating – about 15 minutes.

4 Remove the spice bag and drain the fruit, reserving the liquid. Pack the fruit into warm sterile jars.

5 Pour the liquid back into the pan and bring to the boil. Boil until reduced and slightly thickened, then pour it over the damsons. Seal the jars tightly. Keep in a cool place; once opened, keep in the fridge and eat within a month.

For me, foraging and picking is part of the process in preparing preserves. It is a really gratifying experience and you can work up an appetite being outdoors in the autumn climate.

Spiced Piccalilli and Harissa Paste

The addition of harissa gives this traditional favourite a real buzz! Like most pickles, it is perfect with cheese, especially goats and ewe's milk, such as feta, and a new favourite 'fetys' from Carwyn Adams at Caws Cenarth.

Spiced Piccalilli

Ingredients

2.5kg mixed autumnal vegetables e.g. butternut squash, cauliflower florets, courgettes, leeks, cucumber etc.

120g sea salt

750ml malt vinegar

275g light muscovado sugar

3 tablespoons harissa paste

1.5 tablespoons cornflour

Makes 6 x 340g jars

··

What you do

1 Prepare the vegetables, wash, trim and cut into bite-size pieces and place in a large bowl. Sprinkle with the sea salt, toss through to mix well, cover with a cloth and leave for 24 hours.

2 Drain and rinse the vegetables.

3 Reserve 3 tablespoons of vinegar, mix with the cornflour and set aside. Take a large pan and add the remaining vinegar and sugar, bring to the boil and stir so that the sugar dissolves. Add the vegetables and bring to the boil again, stir in the vinegar and cornflour mix and add the harissa paste, stirring until thickened. Simmer for 8 minutes.

4 Remove from the heat – the vegetables should still have a little bit of a bite to them. Spoon into hot, sterile jars, seal and leave to cool. Keep them in a cool, dark place for 6 weeks to mature, then they are ready to eat. Keep in the fridge once opened.

5 This pickle is perfect with cheeses, a ploughman's or cold meats, especially ham. I also love it as a relish with burgers, hot dogs, bangers and bacon or in a sandwich or toastie!

Harissa Paste

Ingredients

3 tablespoons each of coriander, cumin and fennel seeds

15 garlic cloves, left whole

1 large red onion, roughly chopped

15 long red chillies, deseeded and roughly chopped

1 large red pepper, deseeded and roughly chopped

100ml olive oil

1 teaspoon sea salt

Makes 6 x 340g jars

What you do

1 Make the harissa paste – line a baking sheet with foil, top with the onion, chillies, garlic and pepper, sprinkle with the sea salt and drizzle with 4 tablespoons of the olive oil. Cover with foil and

bake for 25 minutes at 200°C/ Fan 180°C/Gas 6. Remove the foil and roast for a further 15 minutes until everything is soft and slightly caramelized.

2 Meanwhile, dry roast the spices in a hot pan until they become fragrant, about 30 seconds, stirring constantly. Spoon into a spice grinder, whizz to a powder and set aside.

3 Remove the roasted vegetables and pop into a food processor, blitzing to a purée. Heat the remaining olive oil in a pan, add the spices and cook over a medium heat for about 1 minute, then stir in the vegetable purée. Cook for about 20 minutes until it forms a thick paste.

4 Spoon into small sterilised jars and seal immediately. Store in the fridge for up to 4 months. Once opened, add a top layer of oil to prevent mould.

Damson Cheese

This is stunning served alongside a good cheeseboard, it adds a real intensity which cuts through the richness of the cheese. Delish!

Ingredients

1.5kg damsons

750g preserving sugar per 900ml of purée

2 star anise

1 stick cinnamon

6 strips orange, cut with a vegetable peeler

Sunflower oil for brushing

Makes 1.5kg

What you do

1 Rinse the damsons, tip into a large pan and pour enough water over the top just to cover. Bring to the boil, stirring occasionally.

2 The stones will come loose and rise to the surface, remove these with a slotted spoon. Simmer the damsons for 25 minutes, then remove from the heat.

3 Place a sieve over a bowl, spoon the fruit in and push through the mesh with a wooden spoon.

4 Clean the fruit pan. Measure the fruit, pour into the pan and add 750g of sugar per 900ml of fruit purée.

5 Add the start anise, cinnamon and orange. Place the pan on the heat and bring to the boil, stirring to help the sugar dissolve. Boil for about 1 hour until the consistency reaches a thick purée. Stir frequently; when you draw the spoon across the bottom of the pan and you can see it clearly, the damson cheese is done.

6 Brush 6 x 250g foil dishes or jars with sunflower oil and spoon in the purée. Cover with a cut piece of waxed paper or a disc and then clingfilm tightly.

7 Leave to cool completely and store in the fridge for 1 month before eating. This will keep for a year, so would be lovely to serve during the festive season.

If you are lucky enough to have a damson tree, or know someone who has one, this is a great recipe to make. It really adds a concentrated, jammy fruit element to your cheeseboard. I also love it served with charcuterie and roast meats such as porchetta. You can also make this using smallish plums or apples.

The autumn season at the School

September is a busy month for my team; it marks the beginning of the countdown to the end of a busy year. It's like hopping onto a rollercoaster and there is just no slowing down! We have a full schedule of seasonal courses, special events to host and an amazing larder of inspirational produce at our fingertips.

Our recipes reflect the time of year with lots of full-flavoured, slow-cooked dishes such as the Welsh lamb with orange and green olives; complex one-pot wonders like the harvest curry that can be made in advance for later enjoyment and delicious indulgent desserts like prune and chocolate clafoutis.

People also tend to host supper nights at this time of year, so our courses explore menus that can be replicated easily at home and bring something new to the table, such as agnolotti filled with potato, truffle and porcini – all handmade and utterly delicious!

We also host a number of lunch and supper events ourselves, which is a great opportunity to showcase the season and of course do what we love best – inspiring and feeding people!

These events are based on a little club I started back in the mid-90s where I would demonstrate a range of seasonal dishes and then replicate two of them for lunch or supper. It was a great success and quite ahead of its time.

The format became part of the
BBC Wales series *Hot Stuff*, which
was also ahead of its time in terms
of content and the way it was
presented. The title referred to the
hot and happening food scene in
Wales at that time. Each programme
saw me taking a whistle-stop tour
around the country meeting chefs
and producers whilst taking in
the amazing scenery. I would then
return to my kitchen to use the
ingredients and knowledge I had

gathered throughout my travels to
form the basis of a supper party for
friends; it was a big hit!

Back to the present day and we are
about to get busy preserving at the
Cookery School. We plan ahead in
terms of what we are going to make,
so that we have a range of elements
to add to our event menus.

This can include a wild hedgerow
syrup, such as rosehip or sloe,
which can be used in a welcome

drink, a sorbet or dessert or a pickled fruit like damsons in balsamic vinegar with vanilla, delicious with hot and cold meats – cured and smoked – as well as cheese.

The selection for this year has been carefully chosen and I thought it would be lovely to include three of them, plus a spicy paste with serving suggestions.

I hope you enjoy making and sharing these recipes and that they serve you well over the months to come.

Seasonal ingredients

Just look at this list for inspiration!

Vegetables

Aubergines, Beetroot, Broccoli, Chard, Courgettes, Cucumber, Tomatoes, Chestnuts, Calvo Nero, Runner Beans, Spinach, Peppers, Parsnips, Wild Mushrooms, Walnuts, Butternut squash, Borlotti Beans, Cabbages, Cardoons, Cauliflowers, Fennel, Kohlrabi, Pumpkins, Rocket, Salsify, Spinach, Turnips, Thyme, Watercress, Kale, Onions, Celeriac, Celery, Swede, Swiss Chard, Jerusalem Artichokes, Brussel Sprouts, Chicory, Squash and Leeks.

Fruits

Clementines, Apples, Blackberries, Damsons, Greengages, Loganberries, Plums, Cox's Apples, Crab Apples, Pears, Quinces, Rosehip, Sloes, Rowanberries, Elderberries, Figs, Medlars, Cranberries and Satsumas.

Game and seafood

Mallard, Grouse, Guinea Fowl, Venison, Duck, Wood Pigeon, Partridge, Rabbit, Pheasant, Goose, Teal and Hare.

Dover Sole, Brill, Brown Trout, Cod, Grey Mullet, Haddock, Halibut, Herring, John Dory, Mackerel, Monkfish, Plaice, Lemon Sole, Salmon, Sardines, Scallops, Sea Bass, Hake, Turbot, Crab, Clams, Squid, Scottish Oysters, Lobster and Mussels.

Notable dates in autumn

September
Harvest Festivals

October
Halloween – 31 October

November
Guy Fawkes Bonfire Night –
5 November

St Andrew's Day – 30 November

About Angela Gray

Angela opened the Cookery School at Llanerch Vineyard in 2011. The School also hosts a number of special events where Angela cooks, chats enthusiastically and promotes the good life through cooking and eating together.

Everything that precedes her time at the School has given her the wealth of experience and knowledge needed to head such an ambitious project. She worked prolifically in the food world, starting her career as a personal chef working in Europe and North America. Her clients included an esteemed list, from European aristocracy to high-profile clients such as Lord Lloyd Webber. Angela took to the helm at a number of restaurants, where she developed her relaxed style of cuisine with a strong Mediterranean influence.

She returned home to Wales, where her career path changed when she attended university in Cardiff and gained a BSc Honours degree in Food Science. Whilst studying, Angela also ran a small catering business and held a twice-monthly Cooking Club from her home. This would later form the basis of two prime time cookery series for BBC Wales, *Hot Stuff* and *More Hot Stuff*. Next came several series for radio, including *My Life on a Plate* and *Packed Lunch*. She still loves to get involved in media projects, but her main focus these days is at the School and writing her cookery books.

At the close of 2016 the School was listed in the top 10 Cookery Schools in *The Independent*, *The Telegraph*, *Sunday Times* and *Evening Standard*. Most recently it was also chosen for the prestigious *National Cookery School Guide*. In Angela's own words, that's the result of teamwork at its best.

Dedication

For Mike, my family and all of my team, who work so hard to make the School a success. I love you all!

Thanks

To Huw, for all the fun time in the studio making these recipes come to life. A masterstroke once again!

Thank you to Pamela for keeping me in check! What would I do without you?

To Ross, assisting in the studio. What a culinary adventure you have had!

Angela's Recommendations

- Cariad Wine at Llanerch Vineyard.
- Wally's Delicatessen, Cardiff.
- Ashton Fishmongers, Cardiff.
- Paleo Nutrition, Llandeilo.
- Martin Player, Cardiff.
- Halen Môn Sea Salt.
- Dyfi Distillery, Corris, Mid Wales.
- Welsh Whisky Company.

Metric and imperial equivalents

Weights	Solid		Volume	Liquid
15g	$\frac{1}{2}$oz		15ml	$\frac{1}{2}$ floz
25g	1oz		30ml	1 floz
40g	1$\frac{1}{2}$oz		50ml	2 floz
50g	1$\frac{3}{4}$oz		100ml	3$\frac{1}{2}$ floz
75g	2$\frac{3}{4}$oz		125ml	4 floz
100g	3$\frac{1}{2}$oz		150ml	5 floz ($\frac{1}{4}$ pint)
125g	4$\frac{1}{2}$oz		200ml	7 floz
150g	5$\frac{1}{2}$oz		250ml	9 floz
175g	6oz		300ml	10 floz ($\frac{1}{2}$ pint)
200g	7oz		400ml	14 floz
250g	9oz		450ml	16 floz
300g	10$\frac{1}{2}$oz		500ml	18 floz
400g	14oz		600ml	1 pint (20 floz)
500g	1lb 2oz		1 litre	1$\frac{3}{4}$ pints
1kg	2lb 4oz		1.2 litre	2 pints
1.5kg	3lb 5oz		1.5 litre	2$\frac{3}{4}$ pints
2kg	4lb 8oz		2 litres	3$\frac{1}{2}$ pints
3kg	6lb 8oz		3 litres	5$\frac{1}{4}$ pints

Angela's Cookbooks

Angela's cookbooks bring together a collection of recipes inspired by the seasons, her childhood, travels and career in food. They also form the basis of many of the courses run at her Cookery School at Llanerch Vineyard in the Vale of Glamorgan.

Winter Recipes

Everything naturally warms up in colour and flavour in this recipe collection. Angela uses a wide range of ingredients to invigorate the palette, from aromatic spice blends to the punchy flavours of pomegranate molasses, porcini and truffle.

Spring Recipes

Expect fresh, zesty flavours, vibrant colours and lots of inspiring ways to enhance your day-to-day cooking at home.

Summer Recipes

This book features a rich collection of recipes from Angela's travels and her time spent working in the South of France. Barbecuing, dining al fresco, entertaining friends, it's all here.

Autumn Recipes

Colours and flavours become richer and deeper in this book and recipes embrace the wonderful harvest of seasonal ingredients. Angela shares easy ways to entertain so you can be the host with the most.

Festive Recipes

The highlight of the Cookery School calendar is the 'Festive Kitchen' event, where Angela demonstrates a range of inspirational recipes that are all showstoppers, guaranteed to 'wow' friends and family throughout the Christmas and New Year celebrations. This is her very special collection of those recipes.

'There is just so much to be done at this time of year in terms of harvesting, foraging, making, baking, and preserving. At the end of a busy week a little culinary recreation in the kitchen can produce the most delicious comfort food for those cosy suppers together.'